OPEN ME

SABRINA WADSWORTH

OPEN ME

Copyright © Rad Press Publishing
Sabrina Wadsworth
"Open Me"

All rights reserved. No part of this publication
may be reproduced, distributed or conveyed
without the permission of the author.

SABRINA WADSWORTH

This collection is dedicated to
my beautiful daughters
Marie & Sage.

May this book let you know you are not alone
when the hardships in life I can't protect you from
find you.

Love,
Mom

PART ONE
DESERT HEARTBREAKS

OPEN ME

NIGHT TERRORS

Empty journals were not made for only heartbreak;
 they could be filled with the terrors of the night
that are too malicious to be exchanged through lips.

THANK YOU

If it was just me...

Sobriety would always be out of reach
I would never want to try and grab it
I would be alone in my hazy world
I wouldn't want to be anywhere else

If it was just me...

It would be hard to keep my job
I'd live at rock bottom
Nothing would matter
I don't know if I would survive

But now I have you...

I created you and gave you life
I can't be selfish
No choice, but to be sober
And I am all you have to survive

But now I have you...

You deserve the best start
That is the least I can give you
I will do whatever I can for you
You saved me from myself

Thank You

OPEN ME

CONCEPTUAL LOVE

Dear Mister Nice Guy,

   I am sorry,
      But it is true.
   I love the concept.

I don't love you.

OBJECTIFY ME

I feel like I'm going to puke
Since that night was not a fluke
It was as real as can be
And now my true friends I can see

Lamps, pencils, cars, and ships
Mouth, tongue, vagina, and lips
Just an object, nothing more
On your list, an other score

Fun, fun that's all it is
I could be yours, could be his
Not so fun once you know
The baby bump's about to show

So now what do I do
When this is what my life comes to
The choice is mine, it isn't fair
Because none of you even care

Now all I feel is gutless fear
Since you're the ones that put me here

SEPARATE

Right in this instant
You haven't left my sight
Yet you are so distant
Something isn't right

I feel the pain in my heart
As I watch from afar
We are only at the start
Time to wish upon a star

Wish this will be over soon
And back in your arms I'll be
We can snuggle until noon
And love is all we'll see

But right now we separate
Starting with a couple feet
My life is now a life of wait
Until the next time we meet

HER BLACK ABYSS

Horrible deeds done in a horrible spot
She was left naked waiting to rot
A pitiful puddle, a pile of shame
She can't help but think she's to blame
The world is empty, there is no sound
Just his heavy breathing and her fall to the ground
Life has no meaning, nothing to live for
She stays numb in her spot as it begins to pour
Then the sun shines and sheds some light
Makes her cover and close her eyes tight
The back of her eyelids is her black abyss
Empty darkness is her idea of bliss
A savior came and broke past her shield
Gave her a jacket, said she'd be healed
She fully believed, his actions proved true
But when the time came he never pulled through
This savior's a tease, but a persuasive one
She makes herself stay knowing to run
Time to time he will share his love
But when she's in need he gives her a shove
Now in the light she opens her eyes
Smiles for him while her body cries
Happy she is, or so she will say
The truth will come out, it will one day

OPEN ME

CATCH ME

Falling
Harder, faster
Into love

Falling
Harder, faster
Into limbo

INSTANTANEOUS

Reason and love may be distant
But love and hatred come at an instant
They go perfectly hand in hand
So the one you love most
May be the one you can't stand

THE LAST GLASS

The pop of the cork
Pierces the consuming silence
Trickling red velvet
Muffles the desperate sobs

Black tears run down my cheeks
Washing away the beauty
I can't go through anymore
Of life's tortures

Finishing the bottle
A few pills to ease my mind
Clink, cheers, goodnight my dear
I'll be fine

COMFORT

I want to cry the night away
In someone's arms
Knowing they will stay

OPEN ME

PREY

I'll corral you in and you'll come willing.
Your untouched heart
I will be killing.

NIGHT TIME

Hold me close
Snuggle me dearly
Nuzzle my neck
Tangle our fingers
Feel my warmth
Synchronize our breaths
Skip a heartbeat
Fall in love

DEATH

If you keep making my heart skip a beat like this,
I'll flatline.

GONE FISHIN'

You went fishing
Threw out the line
I denied your bait
Even though dIvine

The air is crisp
On this desert morning
I tease, I snag
Without warning

Who would have known
You'd reel me in
And save me from
My life of sin

PERSUASION

Open me up
I'm begging you
Please give me that release

The pressure inside
Is unbearable
I need to feel relief

So grab it
Grab that blade
I promise we will be happy

Yes that's it
The deeper the better
Push harder along me, your vein

I NEED A DRINK

Oh liquor
My best friend
You will forever be

Oh liquor
In the end
It's just you and me

Oh liquor
Fuzzy my mind
Happy my soul

Oh liquor
Make me blind
Devour me whole

KILLING ME

While spoken words damage the heart,
It is the unsaid words that damage the soul.

BREAKING SHELLS

Your love is deadly
And it's killing me

For a seed to grow into a magnificent tree it must be put underground, break apart completely, and release its insides. The shell is destroyed and forgotten about under the earth's soil.

So as I fall apart
Don't be afraid

The seed can only grow with Mother Nature's nurturing. To someone that looks upon this process, ignorant of the results, would see it as complete destruction. That's exactly what it is.

This is what I must do
For us to ever be a two

That's what it has to be for any real growth to happen.

I'll self-destruct and kill the bad
So the great can grow
Let's shine light upon my dark
Watch it disappear and be forgotten
The same as a shell of a seed underground.

LOVE HURTS

A scarf should hide it
This is love
I'm high as a kite
Legs are tangled
I'm yours forever

Morning snuggles
Afternoon picnics
Candlelit dinners
Irresistable to fall for

A minor disagreement
It's ok, I understand
You didn't mean to grab me
I can overreact too

Chocolates and flowers
Overwhelm me with care
You're careful to caress
As you kiss the bruises

Things are well
I know you love me
Just an other bad day
A scarf should hide it

I'll tell my friends
I just tripped and fell
Butterfingers and two left feet
I guess I'm a little clumsy

Now I'm clinging for my life
I'm sorry I said no
At your hands I'm begging
Just love me like I love you

SPECIAL LADY

What, you think you're special?
All pretty and petite
I see the hole in your pantyhose
You ain't that innocent and sweet

I'll treat you how you desire
Your smile tells me how
Six inch heels and darting eyes
Screams you want me now

You walk alone tonight on purpose
So we can have our moment
You turn down a darkened alley
These actions give me your consent

I'll push you down
And I'll pull your hair
I know these are screams of delight
And nothing of despair

Be the good slut that you are
Get on your knees and swallow
You better not say a word
Just live your life in wallow

Go ahead, cry your life away
You got what you deserved
No one cares for little whores
Who pretend they're shy and reserved
What, you thought you were special?

HE'S HUNGRY

Now I'm all alone
Nothing left but fear
Hide from all the windows
Make sure to lock all the doors
Jump when car doors shut
Cower when the walls creak
No one is here to save you
You're just a piece of meat
He is on the prowl
You'll never see him lurking
Adrenaline in your veins
That fight or flight response
In the end he will control you
As you are now
His lonely prey

GOOD NIGHT , I LOVE YOU

I don't want to say good night
Without saying I love you

I don't want to not say I love you
Any moment we part ways

I don't want to part ways
Without saying I love you

If there's ever a chance
I may never say it again

HOLDING HANDS

Lend me your hand
As we enter this place
It's an uncharted land
That's not easy to face

We'll walk through the gates
You'll be drawn in by the stories
Of the happiest fates
And everlasting glories

Your hesitant steps
Become a confident stroll
You've been captured by lust
Who tricks the soul

Then clarity arrives
Realize you're in shackles
This is where pain derives
Haunted by cold hearted crackles

It's ok to be scared
And want to escape
Not everyone is perfectly paired
Instead strangled by their sorrowful cape

But we are still hand in hand
Forever we can be
Let's make our own map of this land
It is worth it, you will see

OPEN ME

One step at a time
Slowly give me your heart
You already have mine
That's a pretty good start

Break free of your chains
Don't let fear control you
Let love reign
Make your life of one, a two

IT'S BED TIME

Just come home
To me tonight
And everything
Will be better

Let your worries
Melt away
Between
These sheets

Look into my eyes
As raw
Carnal desire
Penetrates

Come with me
Help me
Write some
Naked poetry

HEAD GAMES

I just can't
Help but feel
You've gotten
In over your head

Since you have
Surely made me
Head over heels
For you

GREY SKIES

Your world
Is gaining
A somber
Tone

Blue skies
Turning
A forever
Grey

Conversations
Become
A dull
Burden

For every
Hello there's
A Painful
Goodbye

So find
Peace
In your
Solitude

Everyone
Needs their
Quiet
Time

Just don't
Let the silence
Consume
You

When you're
Ready
I am
Here

Grab my hand
We will
Take a
Walk

Together we will
Bring back
Your
Sunshine

A BONE PLEASE

They say guys are the dogs
That only want one thing
Yet right now I would
Beg to differ

Like a dog I'm begging
Just throw me a bone
Like a dog I'm begging
Just tell me I'm not alone

All I ask
Please look my way
Just a glance
Or a simple 'Hey'

'Cause begging is pathetic
And it couldn't be more true
I am fucking desperate
When really I just miss you

Yes I understand
And I'm always here for you
Doesn't change the fact
Sometimes I need you too

Life isn't great with timing
Most times it's pretty shitty
I don't want us to get lost
On the easy path of self pity

So like a dog I'm begging
Just throw me a bone
Like a dog I'm begging
Just tell me I'm not alone

EVIL BLISS

There's a darkness
Inside me
It's been there
For years
A refuge for lost souls
This black hole
Once consumed my life
A flood of light
Is washing over
Saving me
But I won't succumb
To this evil bliss

YOUR LULLABY

This pillow isn't right
These blankets make me cold
The smell of you still lingers
Our memories becoming old

This bed is just too big
For one to sleep alone
This emptiness is scary
These thoughts I must condone

Your body keeps me warm
With my head upon your chest
Your arms around my waist
Put my fears to rest

Every night your heart sings
A soothing heartbeat lullaby
Every night my heart yearns
To listen one more time

KISSES

The sun kisses my skin
But it doesn't
Warm me up

These clothes fit me snuggly
But nothing
Can compare

The air gives me breathe
But it doesn't
Keep me alive

Then there are your kisses
That started a fire
I'll never extinguish

Then there are your snuggles
That let me know
I'm secure

Then there is you
Who gave me
A reason to live again

SUICIDAL LOVE

How fast must I drive
As I turn off the overpass?
What is the best time
To step in traffic?

How deep does the blade
Have to go?
Is it called a jump
When I only stepped off?

How much liquor
Will suffice?
Will these pills
Do the job?

You know I never
Wanted to die
I just wanted to see
Who would care if I tried

How badly must
I be injured
To see if
You'll be here for me?

When I wake up
In the hospital
Who will be
At my bedside?

Will it be your face
I see first
And your hand
Clasping mine?

OPEN ME

Is this what I need to do
To grab your attention?
Is this the extreme I must take
Just to have your affection?

INSANE REALITY

We've been apart for so long
I can't tell if this is real
Are you a reality of my dreams
Or something I'll someday feel?

I have these thoughts in my head
Is that all they'll ever be?
I have these dreams every night
Are you a figment or can I actually see?

All I get is silence from you
So I now have a restless mind
Filled with what-ifs and maybes
Of something I wish to find

But I thought I already had you
You surely do have me
When I handed you my heart
I thought together we would be

Now I'm so confused
What the hell is going on?
Am I overreacting with fear
Or are you really gone?

Is there actually still hope
Or has that ship long sailed?
I can't help but feel
You already have bailed

I can't tell if I am crazy
Or just an average girl
Is this truly real?
Why are you throwing me in a whirl?

In the mean time I'll just sit here
Listening for my phone to ring, I'm waiting
Listening to the insane thoughts
My mind won't stop creating

SUDDEN DEATH

We are hanging
By a thread
I fear our love
Is dead

You show symptoms
Of severe distance
Accompanied by
Painful bloody silence

I have signs
Of constant wonder
Over active thoughts
A growing fear of ponder

Time heals all
But this is sudden death
I just need to know
When did you take our last breathe?

STRIKE OUT

Strike for the heart
Impale it with fear
Your plan from the start
Now the end is here

If you're going to break it
May as well go for shatter
You'll make sure we don't make it
Because to you I don't matter

BUT...

I love you...
But it's not enough
I love you...
But I can't do this
I love you...
But it's too much
I love you...
But you're overwhelming
I love you...
But it's just not the right time
I love you...
But it's not worth it

I love you so much right now...
But it's over

CRACKING CRATERS

What starts out as a crack
Soon turns into a crater
Your words that sound so sweet
Will only kill me later

You came to me with concern
For me and my well being
Yet now my ashes fill an urn
The truth it is you're seeing

While spoken words damage the heart
It's the silence that destroys the soul
So as nice as you may seem this is where we part
For I am someone to never be whole

UNRAVEL ME

I am like a tangled mess of yarn that is just yearning to become a beautiful blanket. Show me some tender love and care and I will unravel into what keeps you warm at night. Love me enough so that I can love you back. Make me into the one thing you reach for at night. Let me wrap myself around you and tuck myself into your crevices. I will comfort you in times of need and soak up any tears. Nightmares will vanish as my snuggles protect you. We can sweat out fevers together and take away the pain. But there will be a day that your blanket will snag. You will remember our past, the desire you once had for such an intricate design, that now may be too much. We will have run our course and you will pull. Unravelling me, leaving me as the tangled mess I truly am.

FALSE HOPE

"I know your past
No one deserves that
I dream we will last
It's as simple as that

Let me prove to you
How you deserve to be loved
Let my actions be true
You'll never again be shoved"

All these words he spoke
I wanted to believe so badly
But I'm fragile, my heart is broke
By one unkept promise sadly

He will never know
I keep this pain as my own
A happy smile I will show
Even though this ocean of tears has grown

BONDAGE

"If you could see yourself
Through my eyes
You would see
How beautiful you truly are"

You raise my hands
Above my head
And tie them
With your touch

Down you go
Silencing me
Gagging me
With your lips

Your sweet seduction
Blindfolds me
From
Reality

The butterflies
Are dying
From your
Poisoned nectar

Now you get lower
Creating mountains
Of goosebumps
On every patch of skin

I'm oblivious
To my shackled ankles
While you sensually
Let your hands explore

OPEN ME

You're bringing me to climax
Okay, I'll release myself to you
A panting breathe of lust
Quickens as I close my eyes

Wait, when did it get so cold?
My eyes are open
Fearful clarity
I'm trapped

I can't see
I can't move
Vulnerable, naked
Truly alone

I hear your voice
Heartfelt promises
Growing distant
Completely disappearing

There is no escape
I can't save myself
I feel your blade
Against my chest

I grit my teeth
You stab my heart
I hold back these tears
You hold it in your hands

"I love you so much right now"
I hold onto your words
As I surrender
My life

Tied up, blindfolded
Gagged, and shackled
If only you could see me
How beautiful am I now?

SELF LOVE

I only like my body when your body is inside of mine.

GREETINGS & GOODBYES

So long my almost lover
Hello my heartless hookup
Goodbye hopes and dreams
Welcome permanent sorrow

Farewell internal happiness
Good morning lonely reality
Until next time innocent giggles
We meet again suicidal emptiness

See ya later mended heart
Hey there crushed confidence
Good night cheerful smiles
Make yourself at home dead butterflies

Come again soon lustful orgasms
Nice to meet you bottle bottom
Have a good life enjoyment
How're you today depression?

YOUR ARMS

Wrap your arms around me
They make me feel so secure
Wrap your arms around me
In our love I am sure

But your arms are changing
You're holding me too tight
But your arms are changing
Impermeable to any fight

Now your arms are gone
These aren't your arms anymore
Now your arms are gone
Just a straight jacket around my core

I MISS ME

You took my hand
And led me away
From this
Consuming darkness

To repay you
For this effort
I began to mend
My tortured soul

I put my trust
In you
As I handed over
My scarred beating heart

Every day since
You have
Taken
A step away

Now you're gone
Disappeared from my life
Ran away to isolation
With my heart

You took my comfort
The only way
I know how to cope
You took my depression

OPEN ME

And now I'm lost
I'm finally happy
Yet utterly destroyed
Because of you

I don't know
Who I miss more
You right now
Or the me back then

A FUCKING GENTLEMAN

I hate you
For every kind word
You ever said to me

I hate you
For the way
You smiled at me

I hate you
For the way your eyes lit up
When ever you looked at me

I hate you
For all the promises
You actually kept to me

I hate you
For the sweet nothings
You whispered in my ear

I hate you
For how gentle
You were with me

I hate you
For making me
Put down the blade

I hate you
For taking away
All of my pain

I hate you
For saving me
From myself

OPEN ME

DAGGERS

You once thought that it was love
And couldn't see the cruel intention
Before you could notice the dagger above,
The kiss of death won the game of temptation

PLEASURE ECHOES

Pleasure
A moment of passion
Exploding ecstasy
Creating a miracle

Love
Brought us here
Trust and compassion
Will keep us here

Magic
A mini us
Inside of me
Growing forevermore

Agony
Contractions between sobs
Blood shedding life
I loved you

Alone
No one is here
Abandoned by you
Stranded in the desert

Empty
No one inside
Just echoes
Of crushed hopes

OPEN ME

PAINTING

Her skin is just a canvas,
waiting for her true colors
to bleed through.

SABRINA WADSWORTH

NAIVETY

Can't believe I'd fall

So hard just to be given

Up on so easy

MARVELOUS MEN

Just bodies in the night
Entering the Keeper of Souls
She's the daughter of the Devil
Devouring these hollow marvels

Modern day Aphrodite
Instilling a need in men
A poisonous, all consuming desire
A fantasy that feels of heaven

Drawn in by her looks
Entranced by her voice
Come kiss away your soul
As if you even had a choice

WHO AM I?

Who am I?
A notch
On your belt
An other lost
Lover

Who am I?
Just a simple girl
Worth no more
Than her
Body

Who am I?
A lonely heart
Just wanting
To be
Loved

Who am I?
A mouth
Two hands
And open
Legs

Who am I?
A forgotten
Drunk, empty
One night
Stand

Who am I?
Your moment
To distract you
From the one
That got away

Who am I?
The fantasy
You can not
Wait to
Fulfill

Who am I?
Whatever you
Want me
To be
Darling

SUNDAY MORNING

"You're amazing at this."
Boy, I've had some practice
Grab my hair, enjoy this bliss
When you leave, this moment you'll miss

Place my lips upon you
Down and up a time or two
Swirl my tongue, this pleasure is true
Can you handle what I'm going to put you through?

Feeling you harden against my cheek
A smile appears, an ending you seek
Open your eyes, take a peek
Capture this view of your little freak

Your body tenses as you let out a moan
I can tell you're ready just by your tone
"Just like that sweety" you passionately groan
So I suck deeper, making this moment my own

It's just your cues I am following
You will never again be wallowing
For your body I am hollowing
The taste of lust I am swallowing

MY TURN

"It's your turn now"
Well then flip me over, show me how
You can be a good lover and keep your vow
After we shall see what I will allow

Start at my neck, you're such a tease
Ah my nipples, go lower, I'm begging you please
Kiss as you go, make me weak to my knees
My heart is racing yet my mind is at ease

I let out a moan, I am speechless
Flick of your tongue, my legs are restless
Lick me, pull me, finger me, I am breathless
Quivering, these orgasms are countless

Let me taste me, give me your fingers
Sweet satisfaction of an orgasm lingers
This ecstasy is blinding, my reality blurs
So lay next to me as my body still purrs

OPEN ME

YOUR BODY

Your eyes
Pierce my soul
Inject me with happiness
Let me see a future

Your lips
Make a unique smile
Flow with heartfelt melodies
Calm me with kisses

Your shoulders
Broad and sturdy
With burdens to bare
Hold a good head above it

Your arms
Wrapped around me
Hold me close
Keep me secure

Your hands
The male match to mine
Grab my waist, turn me on
Caress my cheek, give kisses meaning

Your hips
Push into mine
Pin me down
Deliver us pleasure

Your legs
Strong, muscular, and lean
Walked you into my life
Then carried you right back out of it

DEATH SUCCEEDED

If you keep making my heart skip a beat like this, I'll flat line.

Well that day has come. You took the final pulse to my heart and drained my veins. Now I am alone, wondering. Laying here waiting to see who will take the time to resuscitate me and bring me back to life once more.

FORGET ME NOT

We only have
A few more days
So give me your body
Let me show you my ways

Take off your shirt
Bare me your skin
Unbuckle your jeans
So I can take you in

Go on, relax
I am here to please
Now give me your cock
While I'm on my knees

I will make sure
You never forget
This little red head
You just so happen to have met

GONE TASTING

"Let me taste you
It's half the fun"
You just created a challenge
I have already won

"You're not going to let me?"
No, tonight is about you
"But I want a taste
It will pleasure me too"

Now lay on your back
Get lost in my touch
"So you enjoy this too?"
Maybe a little too much

You're about to give in
Your hands grip my hair
Yet you stop me mid-suck
Before I'm even aware

"You don't understand
This want is a need
Let me go down
I beg you, I plead"

It's funny you think
I'll just let you have me
I'm a delicacy earned
"I'll fight for you gladly"

Pick me up, pin me down
"I'm going to get my taste"
Sneak a smile, pry open my legs
There is no time to waste

Oh God, okay, you win
As your tongue and my clit meet
Please, oh please, don't stop
"Mmm, baby you taste so sweet"

IS THAT NOT A SIN?

At first I felt bad
You were all alone out there
No one to hold you
In the crisp cold air

No brass bars to protect
No glass windows to shield
Just the dangers of creatures
That will hunt you in the fields
I watched with worry
As you spread your wings
In fear of your misery
This chosen life must bring

Then you took flight
No looking back
Then irony hit
Freedom I lack
These bars of brass
Are closing in
You loved me then left
Is that not a sin?

This glass will not shatter
I am trapped watching you
As your life unfolds without me
And your happiness soars true
Every promise you told
And made me believe
Is now another clipped feather

Making flightless wings grieve
"If you're a bird I'm a bird"
Doesn't mean together we will fly
You are up above chasing clouds
I am longing behind glass awaiting to die

SCARLET LOVE

I murdered you
With a blade
I bled you out
Of every vein

I watched you seep
Onto my floor
Your scarlet reflection
Taunting me

With every pulse
Consciousness wanes
As each memory
Of us fades

'Til death do we part
I guess this is it
Just one last breath
Only a few more drops…

I emptied my heart
Painted the ground red
Why do I still love you
When the both of us are dead?

JUST STOP

"I love you"
No,
You just love
The idea
Of love

"I love you"
No,
You just want
To get
Laid

"I love you"
No,
You just are afraid
Of living
Alone

"I love you"
No,
You just think
I'm amazing
In bed

"I love you"
No,
You just want to
Prove to yourself
You can fix me

"I love you"
No,
You just didn't want
To lie
To me

OPEN ME

"I love you"
No,
You are just trying
To convince
Yourself

"I love you"
No,
You just don't
Want me
To leave

"I love you"
No,
You just want
To forget
Her

"I love you"
No,
You just don't
Want to
Regret this

"I love you"
No,
You don't
So stop making me
Believe you

GROWING UP

My faith in love
Is shaken now
And it's all because of you

I've always been
So sure of love
Knowing one day I'll find it true

But then you left me heartless
Even though your last words
Were "Darling, I love you too"

I believed in your kindness
When you promised me
This pain you'd never put me through

Well that promise broke
And here I am
Not knowing what to do

I'm drowning in this hurt
My hope for love is gone
I've gained a cynical view

What is there to live for
If I'll forever be alone
Never again to say I truly do love you

THE DANCER

You waltz into my life
One hand on the door
The other
Reaching for me

No way I can dance
My legs
Are just
Too broken

You give a reassuring smile
With kindness in your eyes
You lift me up
Pull me in

I'm nervous for the steps
It's been long
Since my last
Dance

Here you are just gliding
Every move
Handsome
With ease

Effortlessly you lead
I follow
Seduced by your
Trance

The song drifts off
You bow
And
Leave

OPEN ME

I am wanting more
This you surely know
Being the last true gentleman
That you are

New found legs
A revived heart
I never saw
This coming

Yet here you are
Courting me
One dance
At a time

I'M TRYING

You told me to move on so...

I drowned you in whiskey
I burned you in joints
I lost you in lust

But none of it was working...

I became drunk on your voice
I got stoned off our love
I only orgasmed on thoughts of us

You said I need to let you go, so...

Bottle after bottle
I try to numb the pain
Take a hit and hold it
I try to run away
First dates and hookups
I try to find an other best

But I keep remembering...
The times we drank
Had many firsts
How happy we were
High off each other
The chemistry we had

I fear I will never find again...

THIRD DATE

An accidental brush of arms
Body warmth sparking desire
Star gazing on the roof
Oh how I crave for you to take me higher

Fingers run along my arm
How can you hold a conversation?
As our knees slightly touch
I am put under your sweet sedation

You're cool, calm, and collected
My hands get sweaty as you make the cravings burn
It is a pleasure getting to know you
But now it's your body I want to learn…

LUSTFUL HEARTS

She has
Smooth
Sweet
Skin of silk

He has
Bare
Bashful
Body of stories

She has
Tantalizing
Teasing
Touch of love

He has
Kind
Kinky
Kisses of pain

She has
Lavish
Luscious
Lips of death

He has
Seductive
Sexy
Smile of truth

Together
Happy
Healed
Hearts of lust

HIS MOUTH

Your lips
Capture my attention
Your bite
Has me intrigued
Your tongue
Asks for my affection
Your breath
Leaves me fatigued

Your lips
Get me started
Your bite
Leads me on
Your tongue
Takes me away
Your breath
Brings me back

Your lips
Get me excited
Your bite
Makes me wet
Your tongue
Pulls me over
Your breath
Helps me land

Your lips
Drown me in love
Your bite
Claims me as yours
Your tongue
Devours my will
Your breath
Revives my soul

EROTIC DINNER

I told you today
You're more than welcome
To come over
And have dinner

What I meant was
I want you
Your body
Pressed against mine
Your lips tease my ear
As your breath escapes
And trickles down my neck
Sending arousal down my spine
Just to reach your hands
Grabbing my waist
Pulling me into you
Letting me feel
Just how badly
You want me too
Leaving a trail
Of sexual mountains
Across my legs
That make my toes curl
And a moan release
Feeling the wetness
You create in me
I'm lost in all that is you
One hand inside
The other on my nipple
Mmm you take me closer
Primal moan I give
While your deep thrust I take

Fuck you feel so good
My legs begin to shake
Grab and pull my hair
Bite upon my neck
Bend me over this table
You have me begging for more
Caress my body inside out
Hold me down
And punish me
Teach this angel
The best way there is
To orgasm into sin

But what I said was
What would you
Like to eat
Tonight?

TARNISHED

Here is my body
I gift myself to you
Untarnished skin
Anything you want to do

I don't belong to anyone
Just an ends to a mean
But here you are doing something
That before I've never seen

You treat me with respect
Even though you're wanting more
Invite me out, buy me dinner
Even hold open my door

I expect you to enter
When you drop me off at home
All I get is a kiss goodbye
Surprisingly I'm left alone

Every moment I now ponder
What it is I am to you
Am I someone your heart desires
Or just something you want to do?

Normally I just distract
Guys from their actual pain
But you I reconsider
This may not be a physical gain

When I give you my body
Curious of what you'll do
You tarnish me with hickeys
Claiming I belong to only you

OPEN ME

But nothing is official
I don't know what side will win
Could be just with benefits
Or maybe a relationship will begin

The ball is in your court
This choice I can't decide
But if you desire more
I'll happily be by your side

DEATH OF CHIVALRY

Stop this fairy tale
You're trying to start
There's no way in hell
You'll get to my heart

So take off your shirt
Drop your pants
Fuck me hard
Like it's your last chance

I don't care for chivalry
Or a dozen of roses
Tonight just put me
In climactic poses

I won't be a burden
Just your little whore
Please, I need to cum
I promise nothing more

I'm not clingy for a shoulder
Just hungry for sex
I don't care if there are others
Just when am I next?

LADY LIQUOR

Tonight you are
Coming over
The strongest liquor
Ever made

We brush arms
Your scent
Consumes me
You are potent

Our eyes lock
You shoot me a smile
My first drink
Of the night

My heart
Is getting drunk
Using your love
As a chaser

Knowing in the morning
I will be left
With a hangover
Of false hope

Oh but your touch
Is so persuading
My own mixed drink
Shaken on the rocks

The warm tingle
Of seduction
Dances with my tongue
Deliciously stinging

OPEN ME

The night goes on
Becoming a lush,
From your body
I down an other shot

I drank passed
My limit
You were stronger
Than I thought

The last sips
Were so smooth
You slipped away
Before I could catch

You disappear
With my demons
As I expel them
Down the drain

Only now do I realize
You were my liquor
But I was only
Your night cap

SLOWLY

Time flies fast
But with you it is slow
Our bodies are craving more
Just longing to let go

Such passion is consuming
Two souls lost in lust
I could please you so well
I want is becoming I must

Something holds us back
A simple game of chase
An old lifestyle turned anew
Enjoyably vintage to our time and place

So here we are, naked
A swift movement away
From joining into one
Where in ecstasy we lay

Breathing quickens
Veins are throbbing
Bodies moisten
Innocence our sin is robbing

Yet we go to bed
Two insatiable lovers
Wet against your touch
Tonight we will just snuggle under the covers

KARMA

I said I wanted closure
To help myself move on
My heart has frozen over
I know that you are gone

Your sorry's and your reasons
I could care less to hear
I get it, we are done, it is over
You've made that very clear

I don't need your pity
I can't look weak to you
There's no way you are happy
Knowing what you put me through

May every tear you shed be poison
Slowly killing you over time
Karma will bring my revenge
Punish for this crime

BLURRED LINES

Is this love
Or are we fucking?
Is there even a difference
Like licking to sucking?

I felt your sweet caress
Followed by fingernails
Kisses turn to bites
Leaving seductive trails

Take down my hair
Softly brush behind my ear
Run fingers through then pull
Creating pleasure out of fear

These lines are blurred
Is this sex or being intimate?
Kiss upon my forehead
Are you just nice or purposefully considerate?

I don't care which it is
Just tell me so I know
What am I getting into?
Where is this going to go?

OPEN ME

TINY CURSE

Soft blue eyes,
Freckles on your skin
A seductive smile
Lures me in

Your pretty face,
My fascination
I love the way your body feels
In my imagination

Tonight it's going to happen,
What I dream about since we met
Just the thought of you in me
Makes me wet

The dance of tongues
Removes our clothes
In an ocean of passion
Our lust flows

But soon I realize
I was screwed from the start
The only girth you have
Is a big heart

From now on
You can stay dressed
You're only sexy to look at
It feels so nice to confess

BLACKENED HATE

Surrounded by all this darkness
I am my only friend
Drowning these thoughts in liquor
Rushing to the end

People are all around
I've never been more alone
Soaking myself in poison
Tearing innocence from every bone

Inhaling all this smoke
Trying to burn my soul
May as well put the lighter to my lips
Inside I'm black as coal

Never will I love you
My being is full of hate
Death is soon approaching
I'm no longer worth the wait

MY FLOWER

All I want is love
But settling for lust
My heart has been deserted
Collecting dirt and rust

Every guy I take to bed
An other nail in my coffin
There are no amount of kisses
That can make my dead soul soften

You're the flower on my casket
I'm the thorns to your rose
Bringing hope to the dying
While the pain only grows

A fusion of lips
My lonely fate is sealed
Losing love with every breath
This is death, I can't be healed

GRAVE DIGGER

Like a moth to a flame
I have no control
Flying towards the heat
I've already dug my hole

Men grab your shovels
I'm going six feet under
Buried with every kiss
Fucking to the thunder

Throw roses on my grave
And they will surely die
Wilting with my body
Broken wings cannot fly

Every pound of dirt
Smothers my very essence
No longer will this world
Have to burden my presence

FALSE FOREVER

I am still in love with you
I fear forever I will be
I cannot let you go
I will never set this free

Engraved on my heart
Embedded in my mind
Embracing every touch
In search of what I'll never find

Everyday I'll wait for you
The one that got away
Let me show you my best
Maybe then you will stay...

THE BEGGAR

I was at rock bottom
The day that I met you
My life was such a mess
I didn't know what to do

I said, "keep your distance
I'll only bring you pain."
You told me that I won't
Only happiness we'll gain

I gave you all I had
Sick, depressed me
A month of saying no
Still became a we

You were so determined
A future you were sure
In love with the challenge
Thinking my depression you could cure

Well, darling, you did it
You dug me out my hole
You gave me motivation
Revived my heart and soul

I turned my life around
For me and for you
The day I was ready to give you my best
Was the day that you were through

Told to never beg
But for you my knees are bleeding
I thought I knew you loved me
Just one more chance I am pleading...

INSATIABLE BEAST

This kiss burns my lips
As you push me against the wall
Awakening the beast inside
I've never felt so small

Your hands pin me down
As we move to the floor
The way you move your tongue
"Oh god please," I beg for more

Pull my hair, bite my neck
Bring me to submission
Every move I make
I ask for your permission

Your wish is my command
You have me on my knees
Wet from your pleasure
I've never met such a tease

Bend me over the table
Thrust deep inside
My toes begin to curl
This ecstasy I can't hide

A smile creeps upon your face
You know what is in store
With every muscle, you dominate
Making me your little whore

Insatiable need for lust
Getting off in every position
Passion felt throughout the universe
Energy of stars in a sexual collision

OPEN ME

Two bodies becoming one
Losing oneself in the art of touch
Overwhelming pleasure
Testing the lines of too much

I'm your dirty girl
Make you moan with my tongue
The least I could do
To a man so hung

Tasting your sweet release
As your fingers feel mine
Our bodies collapse together
Succumbing to feeling divine

THE RISING

Every day I wake up
All I see is red
Fed up with it all
Wishing I was dead

No motivation for life
I've already written my note
I'll see you at the river
To a better life I float

The water chills my soul
Shivers bring a wake up call
I am choosing to live
Climbing up from my fall

A mountain of hate
A valley of pain
I will conquer this world
Your submission I'll gain

MY MASTER

I need some direction
My life is such a mess
Please tell me what to do
"Yes, Sir" I'll undress

I am full of lust
Tearing at the seams
Take all my control
Be the man of my dreams
You hold my freedom
With rope I am bound
Tied to the bed
It is love I have found

Punish me
When I do wrong
Your flogger won't sting
For very long
Hold me at my neck
Teach me how to kiss
Pin down my body
I am your naughty miss
Pulling my hair
Bring me to submission
Clarity in my eyes
Let me taste your permission

Put me back together
One spank at a time
Blinded by silk
Our passion is a crime

Throw me down
When you're done
"Thank you, Sir"
For another night of fun

SPRING

In this garden of potential
You have planted a seed
That could blossom for eternity
Or be a disappointing weed

Do I stop you in your tracks
And kill you before you grow?
Or cradle you in my hands
Wait for your true feelings to show?

Will I spend my time in wonder
Of all that we could be?
Or realize my time was wasted
There will never be a you and me?

Knowing all the risks
I still water you every day
Digging my own grave
With hopes that you will stay

You tease me as you sprout
Making plans for our future
Take advantage of my love
Ripping every suture

I talk of all the flowers
All I can do is wait
Only seeing the good
I'm leaving us up to fate

BOOTY CALL

Putting this town behind me
Saying my goodbyes
One last moment with you
Is worth all the tries

You don't have time to stay
I really need to leave
But there's a burning desire
Don't be so naive

Just a kiss farewell?
You silly boy
Let me get a little closer
Tonight we'll just enjoy

Our bodies will entwine
Creating our own ocean
You slip in, down I slide
Heaven in a motion

Lost throughout our waves
You feel me pulse around you
Again and again
I'll let you cum too

I lick my essence off of you
You're my favorite carnal craving
I look up through my lashes
Taste what you've been saving

Deeper into the night
Escape to an other world
Deeper into me
Moaning as my tongue swirled

OPEN ME

You say it's a booty call
Sex without meaning
If that was true, nothing more
It wouldn't leave me feigning

Wanting more, one last kiss
Time has come to part
We truly were two lovers
Destined from the start

BEAUTIFUL DEMONS

You live a life of darkness
Hiding behind the pain
Accepting the death of happiness
Let's open up the vein

Seeing my scarlet reflection
Myself in truest form
This body is getting cold
But the blood is thick and warm

Never thought I'd find comfort
In turning inside out
Serenity in solitude
A self induced drought

Past troubles gave me demons
My thoughts took me to war
I viewed myself as damaged
Rotten to the core

But now I see the truth
Broken skin gave me sight
Embody the gift of darkness
You'll treasure the honest light

Pain is demanding
It shows you who you are
Take pride in your accomplishments
Survival in every scar

To others dark is scary
Demons are unpure
Over time they too will learn
Embracing is the cure

PART TWO
COUNTRY LOVERS

THAT COUNTRY BOY

Every diesel truck
To pass me by
Leaves a rumble
In my heart

Each country song
Reminds me
Of the life
We could start

Every cold morning
Missing your touch
Makes me wonder
Why did we part...

STARRY NIGHT

In the dead of the night
My cigarette spark is growing dim
Sending my hopes up in smoke
My soul is turning grim

Through glossy eyes I look up
In the sky I see your smile
The heat from our explosion
Keeps me warm for just awhile

You are something I can see
But never will I find
You are light years away
In the galaxy of my mind

What we had was beautiful
Destined as a memory
A once in a life time
Supernova of the century

MISSING PIECE

I know that you still care
About this piece of your heart
That I carry with me daily
With this hope, I'll never part

Maybe you'll come back running
Or ask me for my hand
Maybe you see the future
Together like we planned

I know I'm still in love
So you must feel it too
It's been months, you're still debating
To take the risk, become a two

If you ask, I'll jump
For you, I'll do anything
If you want me, I'll come willing
For you are my everything

CURIOUS CAT

Darting eyes
Keep you lurking
Your curiosity
Keeps me smirking

You chose to leave
Cut me out of your life
When days before you wanted me
Forever as a wife

And now you are back
Knocking on my door
Toying with the idea
Of us being more

You're afraid of your feelings
That, I truly pity
Because you know life would be great
If only you were with me

Reality is you're alone
Chasing desperate women
Trying to fill the void
My shoes they'll never fill in

Add an other notch in your belt
For whenever you think of me
Fuck away the pain
Regret is all you'll see

Curiosity kills
I am no longer yours
Satisfaction will bring you back
So for now, enjoy your whores

DESTRUCTION

Before you were so naive
Oblivious to pain
Not knowing of true hurt
When your heart has been slain

I told you I would fix that
Bring you down to my world
The dark to your light
Making all your hopes be curdled

Creating insecurities
Finding all your doubts
I've become your demons
No one can hear your shouts

TENNESSEE WHISKEY

Don't get me wrong
I love my number seven
Jack you're my favorite
But you keep me from Heaven

When the drugs don't cut it
And the sex ain't enough
Gotta do what you can
When life gets rough

That crack of the bottle
Then the pour like rain
Symphony to my ears
Send my life down the drain

Enjoying the ride
To the firey deep
Taking angels down with me
For our souls to keep

I grew up fast
In a living Hell
So wherever I'm going
Will probably treat me well

Straight down my throat
Jack's smoothing the ride
When you're crazy in love
Who cares about pride

What do I do
When the bad looks good
Just to get myself away
I'd do whatever I could

So thank you Jack
Ol' Tennessee whiskey
My life is complete
As long as you're with me

THAT MOMENT

Subtle kisses
Across my shoulder
Fingertips trickle
Down my side

One swift movement
Shedding layers
Letting perky
Nipples show

Flick of a tongue
Hardens and moistens
Dissolving the pain
Within one another

A slow insertion
Creating angelic faces
Healing the voids
That are infecting our souls

CAMPING REINCARNATION

Driving to the woods
Leaving civilization
A breath of fresh air
Becoming a new creation

No social media
No false satisfaction
Just me, myself, and nature
A beautiful interaction

Letting go of maybes
No wasting time in worry
Just floating down the river
Crack a beer, I'm in no hurry

Body in the water
Thoughts up in the sky
The trees filter through them
Time to relax and get high

By myself I am happy
I want for nothing more
Priorities are firewood and fishing poles
Enjoying my time upon the shore

But happiness is only true
When these moments are shared
Maybe one day it will be you
If only you truly cared

OPEN ME

MASKS

I don't even know what happiness is anymore,
I have faked it for too long.

HEADBOARDS

Covering you in velvet
Your hands grab my waist
Forgetting your need to breath
A delectable embrace

Your tongue is my undoing
Gripping the headboard for support
You will finish what you started
I will not let you cut this short

A look of wonder in your eyes
Disappears with satisfaction
Drowning myself onto you
A quivering reaction

Melting into love
Answering my wishes
Set me down gently now
On a bed full of kisses

COMA

Bend me on the pool table
Get in an other score
Forget about compassion
I'm just another whore

Face down, hair pulled
Survival turned to orgasm
I'm so wet, draining tears
My body begins to spasm

This ecstasy is numbing
In exhaustion I am flushed
Escaping this reality
Every feeling must be hushed

Addicted to the coma
Manipulating pleasure
Forever I'm your trash
But once I was your treasure

SUSPENSION

Piercing through my layers
Leaving your crimson mark
Sweep me off my feet
Reignite this spark

Perspective now inverted
Euphoria for the soul
Transforming pain to pleasure
Third eye becoming whole

Now take me to the universe
With the tip of your tongue
Watch as I cross over
Absorb what has been hung

Pure product of passion
Cradle me as I fall
Remove these hooks of love
I have given you my all

OPEN ME

FUCK YOU

For reminding me
Of what it feels like
To be
Happy

LOVE AFFAIR

Baby,
I'll always be there for you
Forever you are mine
Together we are invincible
Surpass the end of time

Sweetie,
It's okay
Let me chase away your fears
Diving into the unspoken
Exposing truths no one hears

Honey,
You're not alone
I'm right here by your side
I see who you truly are
The beauty you try to hide

Darling,
Let me be your savior
No need to just survive
I'll show you what it means
To fully be alive

My Love,
Hold me close
It's you I want inside
I know I'm just a liquor
At least I can say I tried

OPEN ME

WHAT DRIVES US

Instincts;
	Make you search for
  The perfect mate

Hormones;
	Teach you of lust
  And desire

Habit;
	The bad decision
  You never learn from

MOST WANTED

All I wanted was to kiss you
But instead I said goodbye
Never knowing if I'll regret
The fact I didn't try

All I wanted was a hug
But instead I stepped away
Even though I long for you
Each and every day

All I wanted was that look
But instead I closed my eyes
Hoping this dark inside my soul
Can tame these butterflies

All I wanted was to feel
But instead I build a wall
Knowing it doesn't help
It always hurts to fall

All I wanted was to know
But instead I let you be
Hoping one day you'll return
Now that I've set you free

All I wanted was you
But instead I take a drink
Resorting to our memories
I let this heartache sink

OPEN ME

SEASONS

In summer
We thrive
So we fall
Waiting
For winter
To come
And save
Us

TINDER

Making lonely hearts
Be shallow
Through the
Trials of love

Would you fuck 'em?
Swipe right
Secretly wishing to settle
With such a hottie

Needing a rebound?
Drink and swipe
Knowing you'll regret
The instant match

How can one find love
When each first impression
Is laced with the reality
They may just want you in bed?

Who cares for the conversation
Of spoken word
Or actually treasure
Intricate body language?

Did standards of respect
Lower for lack of living up to them?
Or did the supply lessen
Due to lack of demand?

We have lost
The sacrality
Of a genuine
Relationship

UNDER CONSTRUCTION

I knew
I needed
To fix
Myself

I wanted
Us
To
Wait

My
Broken self
Broke
Us

Now
You
Finally
Understand

Because now
You are
Fucked up
Too

FLOODED FAREWELL

To the point of exhaustion
Filled with all your might
Please have your way with me
This is our last night

You try to be selfish
But I just need you in me
Letting the pillow muffle the moans
As you set me free

I lay flat underneath you
You push down the small of my back
Thrusting deep inside me
There is nothing that you lack

Creating the perfect friction
You're making the climb
Smack my ass, quicken the pace
It's about to be your time

But baby I can't help it
Resisting is too much
Biggest mess I've ever made
Releasing every crutch

Better than any drug
A full body euphoria
I'm sorry, I really tried
I promise to make it up to ya

WE ARE ALL PHOENIXES

Swallowing the match
Light the fire that's within
Burning down the girl
Time for the transformation to begin

Floating up in smoke
I have my spirit fly
Leaving my turmoil in the ashes
I rise up to the sky

Now here is a woman
Beauty all throughout
Hair of flames to remember
Never a day without

We all have our own set of ashes
The darkness of the past
We all have our set of flames
This pain won't always last

SOULLESS

I gave away my heart
        Since then
                I've been stealing
            Souls

OPEN ME

WARM ME UP

I finally think I'm ready
To hold an others hand
Take long walks on the beach
Giggle in the sand

Curl up and watch movies
Have picnics in the park
Stay up late exploring
Finding kisses in the dark

Someone to come home to
And talk about our day
Knowing even if it's bad
They are here to stay

False hopes I just imagine
Can't keep my life on hold
I'm moving on, finding warmth
I'm done with being cold

DESPERATION

It's been too long
Since I've been satisfied
These men have arrogance
A false sense of pride

Thinking there is a chance
By an accidental brush of arms
It takes more to get me to bed
Than old country boy charms

But my hands aren't the same
A body I can't replicate
In need of an others touch
Aching to fornicate

Stuck in frustration
Desire turning primal
Giving into instincts
Releasing the animal…

THE OTHER WOMAN

I know
You are with her
Supposedly in love
But I don't think you're sure

I know
I am here waiting
Overcome with lust
Desire is elevating

I know
You feel the same
But are too nice to leave
Who am I to blame

I know
How bad I want you
In every possible way
Oh the things I would do

I know
You want more
Start with a hug
But end on the floor

I know
I'd treat you right
A life of pleasure
No need to fight

I know
It would be incredible
You know
It is inevitable

RED VIPER

Beware of my bite
My poison is deadly
One drop on your skin
A torturous medley

At first I taste sweet
Make you want more
Before you know it
You're dead on the floor

With your heart on my hand
The other on my breast
One last chance to get me off
Only then you'll be laid to rest

On to the next desperate soul
Looking for true love in bed
So come here boy
Let me show you why my lips are red

BOLTS

There's something deep inside me
That just isn't right
Some bolts are loose
Others are too tight

No matter how hard I try
I never will fit in
Time to leave this cage of fear
And embrace what is within

Let this black abyss
Run wild from my soul
There's ecstasy in dying
This pain is devouring me whole

Killing all the butterflies
Only demons can survive
Every day I wonder
If I even am alive

So welcome to my world
Where the sun will never shine
Soulmate to the Devil
This torture is divine

ROXY CABARET

A sea of men
Craving affection
Indulging temptation
Again and again

Downing their liquor
Buying love with tips
Here's an other dollar
Wanting to taste your lips

Can't you see this is a game
Just to pay the bills
False hope it will happen
To satisfy your thrills

SILENCE

I was a light
Slowly fading
Into the deep
Depths of sorrow

Nights grew colder
As my warmth
Was stolen by
Lonesome lovers

It seems as though
I am betrothed
To silent nights
With an empty heart

SABRINA WADSWORTH

ASTROLOGY

You can be my sun and stars
I will be your moon
Together
We will make the world
Go round

FREEDOM

Living in the land of the free
Or so that's what they say
Why won't you let me be?
Do I have to live this way?

All I want is justice
Isn't that my right?
This must be what the consequence of lust is
I should have put up a bigger fight

You walk these streets
As a well respected man
I took all the beats
Surviving? I'm doing all I can

You should be in jail
Rotting like all the rest
Pathetic excuse of a male
How do people only see your best?

My everyday is torture
Yours are filled with glee
My soul has been punctured
See what you've done to me?

You think I enjoyed it
So you did nothing wrong
Any complaint is just regret
Crying wolf is a common song

They say revenge is sweet
I can't wait to taste it
Once your blood and my hands meet
Life will finally be perfect

SABRINA WADSWORTH

TEARS

You don't make me cry
You make me feel like it's okay if I do

Yet, now that I am

You realize what you're dealing with
And regret it

SURE

Are we strong
Enough for this?
I thought our
Love sure was
But now you're fading
Into a mere memory
And there's nothing
I can do to stop it

I need to give you time
Give you a chance
To actually
Miss me
You were so
Adament about us
In the beginning
You were so sure

As soon as I
Believed you
And reciprocated
My affections

You became distant
The future you saw
With us
Diminished

You only want
What you can't have
I guess I should be harder to get
If I ever want to keep a guy
It's hard to understand
How you made me
Fall so hard for you
And be so easy for you to take it back

LIPS

The first kiss
        is the last to be forgotten
The last kiss
        is the first to be remembered

OPEN ME

TRAGEDY

I've caught a case
Of the tragic butterflies
Causing nervous anxiety
Each passing day our love dies

SABRINA WADSWORTH

CHURCH

Silence your mind
Speak with your body
Undress your inhibitions
Unleash your true desires
Leave your place of worship
Indulge my life of sin

WILL POWER

Feeling your eyes on me
Knowing your hands want more
Fueling the flames inside
Craving to be your whore

Whisper in my ear
Goosebumps down my thigh
Fingers graze my collarbone
You're going to make me fly

All my clothes are on
And you already have me dripping
Consumed by your kiss
Lower and lower my hands are slipping...

MUSICAL HEARTS

I found myself dancing
While you sang to my soul
With sweet and succulent words
Creating diamonds out of coal

But there is a song
Embedded deep inside me
A melody of tears
Crying to be free

Fearful, I miss a step
You skip a beat just to match
I tell you I'm about to fall
You extend your arms awaiting to catch

But there is a rhyme
Swaying through my thoughts
Sure this love will bloom
But eventually everything rots

Swooning to your voice
Lyrics from your heart
A rhythm of lovers
My last dance from the start

APPETIZER

You can keep
Your sweet caress
I want your passionate
Drunken mess

A kiss upon my forehead
Is always more than fine
But if you make your way down
Bite my neck, now that's divine

Your lips are sweet like honey
But I would rather
Taste my sugar
Your sticky lips gather

So you can tell me you're in love
Or here just for fun
All that really matters now
Can you finish me that you've begun?

SECRET LOVER

There's a look in your eyes
That makes me bite my lip
Through my lashes I look at you
My purity begins to slip

We kiss, poisonous passion
Your tongue is lethal to my skin
From my mouth, down my neck
My body is wet to let you in

I'm weak to your touch
A simple breath makes me quiver
Kissing your way down
Hidden places get a shiver

Between my legs you look up
Grabbing my waist, I crumble
Toes are curling, eyes roll back
Fuck me please I mumble

You bring me to the edge
Then stop just before
Your sinister smile shows
As you hear me beg for more

Oh how I want you in me
And feel how deep you go
Make me scream your name in pleasure
How I feel as I cum is what I want you to know

You try to stay a tease
But you took my body too far
Boy I know you want it too
Let me take you to the stars

You try to hold me down
But you can't control my hips
Arms are pinned but my legs wrap around you
One thrust up and in me you slip

A gasp released, all frustrations gone
A fantasy finally becoming true
Fingernails digging in
For me that's number two

Your thrusts pick up pace
Your body starts to tense
Just as you're about to
I move and leave you on the fence

You start to think I'm mean
Trust me that isn't true
On my knees I go
I just want to taste you too

MIDNIGHT DREAMS

I never knew of sweet dreams
Until you wrapped your arms around me
A surreal calm in the night
Your breathing can be

You make me surrender
Drift off to wonderland
At mercy to your kiss
Hostage to your hands

Your heart beats upon my cheek
Fingers tussle through my hair
Nuzzled into my neck
Throwing me into despair

I've never been more comfortable
To be lost between these sheets
This passion is explosive
We are burning from the heat

The moon becomes the sun
Floating even higher
Falling down into slumber
Time stolen by desire

HEARTLESS

You say I have a heart
That's just behind some walls
Honey that ain't true
Love doesn't make the calls

Inside me I am empty
No hearts can survive
Try as you must
There is nothing to revive

Just a hollow cage
Lined with shallow nights
Temporary lust
Avoiding all the bites

Many that have tried
Will tell you it's a fact
There is no future of us
For it's a loving heart I lack

DEATH DATE

When we kissed
You took my breath
Sweat of our passion
Drowned me
Teeth biting
Pieces of my soul
Hickeys creating
A tattered body
Fingers steal
Any dignity I had
With your body
You tortured me

It wasn't until
You said goodbye
That I actually
Died

FIREBALL

Red hot down my throat
Fire in my soul
Leaving my body to char
A sinful tattered coal

Tasting of candy
This cinnamon kerosene
Turning pain into pleasure
Whiskey ain't so mean

It hurts to look good
That's how ladies are raised
Give me an other burning shot
Let lowered inhibitions be praised

Dancing with the devil
I ask if you're around
May as well make a home in hell
It's nice and warm underground

COMICS

Are you my villain?

Killing any
    Sense of happiness
Murdering each
    Innocent dream
Poisoning
    Every hope
Preparing me
    For my demise
Riddening my world
    With evil?
Or
Are you my hero?

Flushing out
    My demons
Having faith
    In my strength
Challenging
    My fears
Uplifting
    Damaged spirits
Reviving the chance
    Of a future
Making me
    Fall in love?

ANATOMY

In dark depths
With a cage of white
Bloody walls
Hold in this heart

A prison of pain
Shackled by fear
There is no future
If there is no escape

Slipping through the gaps
Finding freedom
A life destined
Of torture

ZOMBIE

I ripped
My heart
Out of
My chest

My
Treasure
Your
Garbage

Somehow
I am
Still
Alive

No wonder
Why
I feel
So empty

SUBLIME

Grab
Break
Pack
Hold

Angle
Flick
Burn
Inhale

Hold
Relax
Exhale
Pass

Feel
Absorb
Enjoy
Love

COMPROMISE

I want to be happy
But not
Without
You

I feel bad laughing
When we
Aren't
A two

I dont understand
What you're
Going
Through

But don't you see
That I am
In pain
Too?

DISCONNECTED

Why can't we talk?
I never did you wrong
Was I just a girl
You enjoyed to string along?

To you I'm just a girl
To me you're my forever
I'm just one of your many
I'll never find someone better

OPEN ME

MISTAKES

Addiction
Life obsession
Main priority
Excessive amounts

High Drive
Persistant desire
Above average
Forever climbing

High Tolerance
Needing more
Low levels
Broken receptors

Fucked Up Hormones

LIFE JACKET

Across the waves
I set sail
This hidden truth
I will unveil

You're my mystery
My deep ocean blue
The moon's pulling us closer
What are you gunna do?

If I go overboard
Will you try to save me?
Throw me a rope
Or anchor me to sea?

You're my mystery
My deep ocean blue
The moon's pulling us closer
What are you gunna do?

My heart's becoming ice
With each moment that I wait
Death to the ship kills the captain
The hunter's become the bait

You're my mystery
My deep ocean blue
The moon's pulling us closer
What are you gunna do?

NYMPHOMANIAC

I
    have so many
    memories
    to get me off
    at night
Can't
    seem to choose
    from my collection
    anyone
    but you
Get
    back
    in my life
    or
    in my bed
Enough
    of all
    these
    stupid
    games
Sex
    is
    all
    we'll
    ever need

BLACK & BLUE

Your words are so malicious
But your lips taste delicious
How can you be so bitter?
Making love just to hit her

Stayed by you for so long
She's never done you wrong
To you she was nothing more
Than a beaten down, fucked up whore

She was an angel that has fallen
A little far from her callin'
Finding herself through the slums
Creating the beat of her own drums

The only day you'll see her light
Is when you see yourself in the night
See the devil that you are
And how purity can have a scar

THRILLS

The
      wrong
            looks
                  good

The
      bad
            tastes
                  right

Take
      away
            the
                  pain

Give
      me
            the
                  light

KICKED TO THE CURB

Dining in the dumps
Taught me of dirtbags
Ecstacy in pain
Taking an other drag

Numbing myself to feel
The nothing inside you
So I can have a hole
Inside my chest too

Men challenge the wound
The gentlemen aim to last
But before I bleed out
They soon become the past

Looking at their skeletons
All men are the same
Some are sweet, some are mean
But each one plays the game

Reaching for the light
Infected by every kiss
Maybe a life alone
Is the only chance for bliss

THAT FIRST KISS

Right hand:
      collarbone
      neck
      nape
      hair
Left hand:
      waist
      hip
      back
      cheek

Chest to chest
Brushing knees
Leaning down
Tipetoe stand

Relax the eyelids
Race the heart
Take one last
Breath...

SABRINA WADSWORTH

FINALLY

You're
      A master
      Of the art
The
      Green thumb
      Of darkness
One
      That can grow
      Flowers in Hell

ROLLING STONES

Pain damaged your soul
Turned you into stone
A mountain high of fears
Is all you have grown

Rolling down the mountainside
Scared to collect moss
Controlled by your demons
Created after loss

Baby, I am rolling too
Life has become a blur
After I lost him
After you lost her

But if we descend together
Each other we'll see clearly
Roll with me now
Let us love dearly

MATRIMONE

The butterfly
With charred wings
Finds the flower
With no petals

Unstable
Discombobulated
Irrevocably
Dissheveled

With different tortures of the mind,
Can this existential idea of love
Exist between two twisted, broken hearts
Ridden with worrisome doubts?

OPEN ME

STAND

You want to know how long it takes
For something new
To become used?

One night.

SABRINA WADSWORTH

FACE DOWN

Do I fight or give in?
Spitting bloody tears
Is it over or just begin?
Destruction is all she hears

Every 'I love you'
A scar on her wrist
If only it was love
Behind every kiss

CHILDHOOD

I miss the days
        Of climbing trees
        Finding ways
        To get that
        Sober high

Now happiness
        Is only a
        Superficial bliss
        I want to believe
        But it will always be

              A lie

SABRINA WADSWORTH

FIFTY ONE FIFTY
In
The end
Death will win
So may as well
Make it on
My terms

OPEN ME

Never settle for mediocre love, sex, or burritos.
　　　　　-Sabrina Wadsworth

PART ONE : DESERT HEARTBREAKS

Night Terrors	9
Thank You	11
Conceptual Love	13
Objectify Me	15
Separate	17
Her Black Abyss	19
Catch Me	21
Instantaneous	23
The Last Glass	25
Comfort	27
Prey	29
Night Time	31
Death	33
Gone Fishin'	35
Persuasion	37
I Need A Drink	39
Killing Me	41
Breaking Shells	43
Love Hurts	45
Special Lady	47
He's Hungry	49
Good Night, I Love You	51
Holding Hands	52
It's Bed Time	55
Head Games	57
Grey Skies	59
A Bone Please	61
Evil Bliss	63
Your Lullaby	65

Kisses	67
Suicidal Love	68
Insane Reality	70
Sudden Death	73
Strike Out	75
But...	77
Cracking Craters	79
Unravel Me	81
False Hope	83
Bondage	84
Self Love	87
Greetings & Goodbyes	89
Your Arms	91
I Miss Me	92
A Fucking Gentleman	95
Daggers	97
Pleasure Echoes	99
Painting	101
Nativity	103
Marvelous Men	105
Who Am I?	107
Sunday Morning	109
My Turn	111
Your Body	113
Death Succeeded	115
Forget Me Not	117
Gone Tasting	118
Is That Not A Sin?	121
Scarlet Love	123
Just Stop	125

Growing Up	127
The Dancer	128
I'm Trying	131
Third Date	133
Lustful Hearts	135
His Mouth	137
Erotic Dinner	138
Tarnished	140
Death Of Chivalry	143
Lady Liquor	144
Slowly	147
Karma	149
Blurred Lines	151
Tiny Curse	153
Blackened Hate	155
My Flower	157
Grave Digger	159
False Forever	161
The Beggar	163
Insatiable Beast	164
The Rising	167
My Master	169
Spring	171
Booty Call	172
Beautiful Demons	175

PART TWO : COUNTRY LOVERS

That Country Boy	179
Starry Night	181
Missing Piece	183

Curious Cat	185
Destruction	187
Tennessee Whiskey	188
That Moment	191
Camping Reincarnation	193
Masks	195
Headboards	197
Coma	199
Suspension	201
Fuck You	203
Love Affair	205
What Drives Us	207
Most Wanted	209
Seasons	211
Tinder	213
Under Construction	215
Flooded Farewell	217
We Are All Phoenixes	219
Soulless	221
Warm Me Up	223
Desperation	225
The Other Woman	227
Red Viper	229
Bolts	231
Roxy Cabaret	233
Silence	235
Astrology	237
Freedom	239
Tears	241
Sure	243

Lips	245
Tragedy	247
Church	249
Will Power	251
Musical Hearts	253
Appetizer	255
Secret Lover	256
Midnight Dreams	259
Heartless	261
Death Date	263
Fireball	265
Comics	267
Anatomy	269
Zombie	271
Sublime	273
Compromise	275
Disconnected	277
Mistakes	279
Life Jacket	281
Nymphomaniac	283
Black & Blue	285
Thrills	287
Kicked To The Curb	289
That First Kiss	291
Finally	293
Rolling Stones	295
Matrimone	297
Stand	299
Face Down	301
Childhood	303

Fifty One Fifty 305

ABOUT THE AUTHOR

Sabrina Wadsworth weaves pain and taboo into a heartfelt collection for her readers. She is a single mother of two amazing daughters. The three of them live in Northern California in a quiet valley countryside. She enjoys meditating through her daily yoga practice. Sabrina is a full-time college student. She has her Associates Degree in Applied Sciences and is currently studying towards her Bachelors Degree in Psychology. Upon graduation, Sabrina plans on continuing her education and pursuing a Master's Degree in Midwifery to become a Midwife.

When not wrapped up in school, work, or family, Sabrina thoroughly enjoys her alone time. If she isn't writing, Sabrina is most likely to be crocheting or staying up late just to watch the stars.

Follow her journey on Instagram @SomeYogaLovin.

www.ingramcontent.com/pod-product-compliance
Lightning Source LLC
Chambersburg PA
CBHW032028290426

44110CB00012B/716